BIG ORANGE

WISDOM

BIG ORANGE WISDOM

*The Story of Tennessee Football
Through the Voices of the Players,
Coaches, Fans and Media*

By
Alan Ross

WALNUT GROVE PRESS
Nashville, TN 37211

ISBN 1-58334-036-X

The ideas expressed in this book are not, in all cases, exact quotations, as some have been edited for clarity and brevity. In all cases, the author has attempted to maintain the speaker's original intent. In some cases, material for this book was obtained from secondary sources, primarily print media. While every effort was made to ensure the accuracy of these sources, the accuracy cannot be guaranteed. For additions, deletions, corrections or clarifications in future editions of this text, please write WALNUT GROVE PRESS.

Printed in the United States of America
Cover Design: *Bart Dawson*
Typesetting & Page Layout: *Sue Gerdes*
Back Cover Photos (l to r) — Tee Martin, Johnny Majors, Peyton Manning:
University of Tennessee Sports Information Department

1 2 3 4 5 6 7 8 9 10 • 99 00 01 02 03

ACKNOWLEDGMENTS
As always, thanks Cris. I'm loving the journey.

To Karol, whose devotion to our love is as vast and encompassing as her dislike for sports in general.

Special thanks also to the magnificent staff at Walnut Grove Press, whose tireless efforts make it all happen.

For
Johnny Majors, Mallon Faircloth, Richmond Flowers,
Bobby Majors, Haskel Stanback, Condredge
Holloway and the other Vol heroes I grew up with

Other WALNUT GROVE PRESS Books
by Alan Ross

A Brief History of Golf
Echoes from the Ball Park
Hooked on Hockey
Golf à la cart
Wildcat Wisdom
Total Soccer

Non-Sports Titles

Love Is Forever (co-written with Karol Cooper)
The Lure of Lighthouses

Table of Contents

Remembrance

Televised college football in 1956 wasn't the cornucopia of satellite selection available today. One game, usually a regional broadcast, was carried in the East by a local station and that had to suffice, though it hardly quenched the fires of pigskin passion for a 12-year-old.

Stuffed with my fill of Boston College, Holy Cross, Army, Syracuse, Yale, Colgate, it was with real curiosity that I wondered about names I'd only read about — Oklahoma and its will-o'-the-wisp halfback Tommy McDonald, Texas Christian with All-America Jim Swink...and a magician tailback from the South, from Tennessee, named Johnny Majors. Even his name sounded cool. When Collier's magazine dedicated a massive spread to its 1956 All-America team, the sight of McDonald in red on one page and Majors in bright orange on another stole the breath of youngsters unknowingly in search of icons.

The only glimpses of Majors back then were on newsreel highlights at the movie theatre. Five years later a sophomore tailback with another cool name, Mallon Faircloth, erupted on the UT scene and wound up eclipsing Majors in career all-purpose yardage.

My Tennessee heroes continued to emerge. There was Richmond Flowers in 1966, following UT's celebrated out-recruiting of Bear Bryant for *the Alabamian's world-class two-sport services. Later there were the familial footsteps of Johnny's brilliant younger brother, All-America safety Bobby Majors, and the justified ballyhoo of Haskel Stanback's arrival on the UT campus in 1970.*

My alma mater, Fordham, and UT even have some history together. It was Fordham that was rumored to be luring Tennessee's natural treasure, head coach Robert Neyland, away from UT back in 1932. The General acknowledged that an attractive offer had indeed been tendered, and Tennesseans everywhere assumed his departure was imminent. But the greatest coach in Vols history showed his blood ran true orange when, with no pay increase from UT's Athletic Council, he chose to remain on The Hill. Fordham, in the first-ever meeting between the two schools two years later, on Nov. 3, 1934, edged Tennessee 13–12 in New York — one of only two losses suffered by the Vols that year. The two met just one other time — eight years later, in 1942, in Knoxville. Payback time. UT flattened the Rams 40–14 while The General was away on active military duty.

My attachments to Tennessee, then, come honestly — right through the fan's front door. Even a boy from the hills of southern Connecticut in the mid-Fifties could not escape the mysterious hold and surprising reach of the great orange tentacle that is Tennessee football.

a.r.

Introduction

I've always felt football should be fun. That glib oversimplification extends more to my reading and writing on the sport these days, at 54, than the actual playing of the game.

My high school and limited college playing experiences, as lackluster as they were, will continue to be cherished by me alone for reasons bordering on the morbidly sentimental.

But when I read about football, I'm continually in hopes that fun things will fill the pages that I'm looking at; that it might even excite my restive grey matter.

That's what I hope I've accomplished with *Big Orange Wisdom*. It's presented largely through the voices of the many legends, heroes, contributing athletes, fans, and media members that have coated an entire state the color of orange, one brush stroke at a time.

Fun for me is writing about the great players, the great teams, the great coaches, the great moments, the great rivalries, the great tradition, the great fans. It's all here, the whole orange crate, from Floozy Loucks' first UT pass in 1906 right up through the 1998 national champs.

Happy Big Orange picking.

The game of football is beginning to obtain a foothold here.

Knoxville Journal
November 20, 1891

Chapter 1

Origins: Early Inklings of Orange

First UT Football Game

The University of Tennessee played its first intercollegiate game of football, on November 21, 1891, against Sewanee, in Chattanooga.

Ex-Princeton player H.K. Denlinger, hired by UT to direct its athletic program, was coach, star, and...professor! A comment in the *Knoxville Journal* on the eve of that first game appeared to have been a harbinger of things to come.

"If we are routed," said the *Journal*, "we will send our baseball team down next spring to balance up accounts."

Give the paper points for peerless prognostication. Tennessee was whitewashed 24–0. About 100 spectators attended the game, after which "all of the boys took in the theater."

Sewanee, a true Southern powerhouse, owned UT in the first four games between the two. Going into their fifth meeting, the Tigers' cumulative score versus the Orange and White was a deflating 139–0.

Tennessee finally overcame its Goliath-like foe on November 1, 1902, with a 6–0 victory.

First Football Win

Tennessee did not claim its first gridiron victory until the 1892 season opener at Maryville, where the Orange and White took a 25–0 win. The victory evened Tennessee's cumulative record at 1–1. It would be another five years before they would reach the .500 mark again.

Another noteworthy event took place in that same season. UT's long intrastate rivalry with Vanderbilt began with a 22–4 loss to the Commodores.

In those days, four points were awarded for a touchdown, two for the conversion after a touchdown, five for a field goal, and two for a safety.

The State of Football's Popularity — 1902

The same year that Tennessee registered its first-ever victory over Sewanee, the Orange and White traveled to Atlanta, on November 22, 1902, to play rugged Georgia Tech. Five hundred fans witnessed a Tennessee comeback in the closing minutes of the game that gave UT a 10–6 win.

That same day in New Haven, Connecticut, 30,000 people watched Yale dismantle Harvard 23–0.

None were killed. In addition to the injuries sustained by Miller and Peters, Spence was bruised about the face and French had a tooth disturbed.

> *Anonymous newspaper account*
> *of UT's 12–4 win over the Knoxville YMCA,*
> *November 29, 1894*

The cannons were rolled from their sheds and fired 16 times in honor of Tennessee. Then the rattle of musketry commenced, lasting for an hour, after which the women students sang songs of victory.

> *Knoxville Sentinel,* November 12, 1899,
> *after Tennessee's 5–0 victory over Georgia*

We played three games in eight days. In that third game we had but 10 players and Coach Dupree had to play fullback for us.

> *Tom Ragsdale*
> *UT guard-defensive back (1905, '06), on 1906 Vols squad*

Subsequent to the call for a cognomen for the Tennesseans, one of the admirers of the old school has suggested "the Volunteers." The name sounds good, and it is likely that it will stick....All hail the Volunteers!

> *Knoxville Journal,* March 25, 1905

How Tennessee Got Its Nickname

The proverbial call to arms and a determined people's overwhelming response to that call over the years has earned the homeland of Tennesseans renown as the Volunteer State.

In the War of 1812, under the command of Andrew Jackson, Tennessee volunteers put down the Creek Indian uprising and participated in the Battles of Pensacola and New Orleans. Later, at the outset of the Mexican War, Tennessee Governor Aaron V. Brown issued a call for 2,800 fighting men. Over 30,000 responded.

The association of the University of Tennessee and the name "Volunteers" was first put together in a story appearing in the *Atlanta Constitution* after the 1902 Tennessee-Georgia Tech football game. It is likely that the newspaper made the link between the two because the game landed in a time frame closely following another war, the Spanish-American War of 1898.

It wasn't till the spring of 1905, though, that the nickname became fully adopted.

When you "made" the team you were officially known to be the best man for that position; hence were expected to play every minute of every game. There were no huddles, and no time out for anything except injuries. When taken out, a player was out for good. Hence an injured player was never removed until at least two buckets of water, liberally sloshed over the fallen warrior, failed to bring him back to life and a desire for further combat. I don't know why we all didn't get killed.

Benton White
UT letterman (1907, '08)

So tight was the budget — get a load of this — we often had to play *two* games on a weekend road trip! We would play Georgia Tech in Atlanta on Saturday; drop over to Athens and play the University of Georgia on Monday. Or play Mississippi A&M (now Miss. State) in Memphis on Saturday and the University of Arkansas in Little Rock on Monday. We did this with 13 or 14 men. Those laments about the "tough" schedules of modern teams often leave us old-timers unimpressed.

Benton White

I'm sure that the first Tennessee pass was thrown by our quarterback, "Floozy" Loucks.... I am quite certain he was the one who threw it (in 1906) because our quarterback did almost all the passing....Of course no one had any past experiences in pass defense in those days.

Nathan W. Dougherty
Vol football captain (1909)
and former Dean of UT College of Engineering

Most of the players nowadays would refuse to play with the equipment available then and on the football fields like the champions of 1914....The boys had one uniform for games and practice; the only padding was sewn into the shoulders and elbows....Face masks had not come into being, but we did have nose guards. But they were held in the mouth and did not give full and complete protection, because they could be knocked aside and they also interfered with breathing.

Zora Clevenger
UT football coach (1911-15)

Our team never thought about losing —
their only thought was "How much do
you think we'll win by today?" This
spirit to be a winner is one that every
man needs in the game of life. The
hardest blocks and tackles come after
graduation.

Malcolm Aitken
captain, 1932 Vols

Chapter 2

Life Lessons

If you ever get your chance, take advantage of it. Be ready to play when you're called on. Take advantage and do your best.

George Cafego
legendary Vol tailback (1937-39)
and two-time All-America (1938, '39)

When I go out on a football field, I feel that I'm the best on the field. I have always considered myself a winner. If you believe this and can get it across to the other players, they believe in you and pretty soon they believe more in themselves.

Dewey Warren
Vols star quarterback (1965-67)

Winning is what the game of football, and life, is all about. When you teach the winning philosophy to a football squad, you are also answering some of the "whys" these people will succeed in the life ahead.

Bill Battle
UT head coach (1970-76)

My freshman year in high school, I was 5-2 and weighed 119, and I played trumpet in the band. We marched at the games. I didn't care at all about football. I ate hot dogs and looked at the girls. Then I changed high schools. I didn't have any friends in the new place....Then one day a girl walked up to me in the corridor and told me that if I went and got a crew cut maybe some of them would start talking to me....Well, I hightailed it down to the barbershop and came back with a crew cut that apparently made me acceptable enough so that I was invited to the weekend high school dance. Well, that night I got into a fight. I was leaving the place with a girl who was a cheerleader. A big guy, a *huge* guy, about 6-8, came running out and wanted to know what I was doing taking his girl home. He grabbed me. Out of fright I swung a punch at him, and down he went, right there on the street under the arc light. I reached down and grabbed his jacket, and he busted out crying and carrying on and asking me to leave him alone. This huge guy, and all of a sudden here he was on the ground. Well, I got this tremendous surge of confidence. After that, I didn't play trumpet anymore. I didn't even know that football existed then, but I would guess that knocking that big lug down put me on the road to it.

John Gordy
All-SEC tackle, UT captain (1956)

Defensive back? It makes a man out of you. You're just a sissy when you're a receiver. I got to be a man *and* a sissy.

> *Richmond Flowers*
> *Vols star wingback (1966-68)*
> *(note: Flowers was not converted to defensive back*
> *until he was with the Dallas Cowboys in 1969)*

A receiver runs forward, a defensive back runs backward; receivers don't want to be hit, defensive backs *have* to hit. It's entirely two different mindsets. It showed me you can do whatever you set your mind to do. You see defensive backs become receivers, but how many times do you see receivers become defensive backs? In my life I've realized you can *make* changes. You have to work. You may have to lay another foundation, but you can do it.

> *Richmond Flowers*

Having to go through all that uproar about being the first black quarterback in the Southeastern Conference prepared me for a lot of things. It wasn't easy, but I handled the situation. My mom and dad, Condredge and Dorothy, really prepared me for that and got me through it. Strong family ties are a must.

Condredge Holloway
star UT quarterback (1972-74)

Playing football at UT gave me a very bright outlook on life and what can be achieved if you take care of your own business.

Condredge Holloway

The education of so many young people through football is vital to our society.

Bill Battle

Live in your hopes and not in your fears.

Johnny Majors
all-time Vol tailback (1954-56), head coach (1977-92),
All-America and Heisman runner-up (1956)

Fear the worst, while hoping for the best.

Part of General Robert R. Neyland's philosophy

By going against the best, it will only make you better.

Randy Sanders
quarterback (1985-88),
assistant coach (1989-)

You've always got to have a shred of hope.

Spencer Riley
junior guard,
Vols 1998 national championship team

What we need to do right now is prove a big point.

Kelly Ziegler
linebacker (1984-87, Co-Capt. '87),
before 1986 Sugar Bowl upset of Miami

T he lessons learned upon the football field are carried usefully from the field into life. It has been said that there is guts at both ends of a bayonet. Well, there is guts, too, at both ends of a tackle. The tired and battered boy who schools himself to throw a shoulder at the thrashing knees of a fullback learns something which of necessity must remain foreign to the player who sits upon the bench for 58 minutes and trots out to lift a long punt.

Gen. Robert R. Neyland
legendary Vol head coach,
(1926-34; 1936-40; 1946-52)

Tennessee football *is* Tennessee.

Winfield Dunn
former governor of Tennessee

Chapter 3

Tradition

Tennessee football means Gene McEver, Bobby Dodd, an incredible streak of 62-1-5 between 1927 and 1933, Beattie Feathers, Bob Suffridge, John Majors, Bob Johnson, Dick Huffman, Walker Leach, and scores of others cherished in memory. It means exhilarating victory over Alabama, galling defeat by Archie Manning and Ole Miss, frustrating disappointment in many bowl games, Hall of Fame honors for eight (now 18) super standouts, cruising down polluted Lake Loudoun to the games, breathers that nobody wants and an incredible loss to Chattanooga and subsequent riot, brunches and missed kickoffs, cocktail parties and hangovers, midnight calls for coaches, the heartbreak of firing and the thrill of hiring and starting anew.

Tom Siler
sports editor, Knoxville News-Sentinel,
1970

Football isn't a sport around Knoxville — it's a religion. The Tennesseans will follow Cafego and Butler and Molinski and Foxx and all the other Vols with the faith of a sawdust convert.

Henry McLemore
United Press
Dec. 12, 1939

Dixie plays for blood. The Tennesseans are ready. Major Neyland knows it.

Fred Russell
Nashville Banner, Jan 1, 1940,
UT vs. USC in the Rose Bowl

Tennessee is Tennessee and rich in tradition.

Frank Broyles
former University of Arkansas head coach
and TV commentator

Tennessee's football tradition is minimizing mistakes.

John Bibb
sports editor, The Tennessean,
Dec. 29, 1985

All people watching TV need to see is the checkerboard (end zone), and they know that Tennessee is playing at home.

Bud Ford
Vols assistant AD for sports information

Our band plays *Rocky Top* at least 20 times a game, though I'm sure our opponents would put that number closer to a hundred.

Bud Ford

Another Tennessee Vols tradition: *vol*ume.

John Walters
writer

Dickey Does It

When Doug Dickey became Tennessee's head football coach in 1964, he instituted several innovations that have become part of vintage lore at UT:

- Introduction of the checkerboard end zone at Neyland Stadium.
- Placing the orange *T* on football helmets.
- Players entering the field through the human *T* formed by the Pride of the Southland Band.

As a rule, pre-game pep talks do more harm than good. Inspiration at zero hour is a poor thing to rely on. Good mental attitude the day of the game stems almost entirely from attitudes built up over a long period of time.

Gen. Robert R. Neyland

Chapter 4

Game Day

It is a stout-hearted boy who can stand the strain of preparation for a classic and step on the field without a small elevator of ice running up and down his spine.

Fred Russell
Nashville Banner, Jan. 1, 1940,
the day of the UT-Southern California Rose Bowl game

I wonder if Tennessee might change tactics and kick off instead of receive if it wins the toss (in the upcoming Rose Bowl). Under tension, you know, it is better to give than to receive, and Tennessee really can.

Fred Russell
Nashville Banner, Jan 1, 1940

The more I am involved with football, the more I believe emotions control the outcome of most games....How ready a team is to play sometimes means everything.

Bob Johnson
UT all-time center and two-time All-America (1966, '67)

Knock a man down, and if you can't, step aside and let me through.

Gene McEver
legendary Tennessee halfback (1928, '29, '31),
All-America (1929)

One Tennessee assistant told me that Hank Lauricella has thrown at least 5,000 passes since the season-ending game with Vanderbilt.

Raymond Johnson
Nashville Tennessean, Jan. 1, 1951,
commenting on Lauricella's preparation
for 1951 Cotton Bowl game vs. Texas

I feel like the Christians must have felt before they let the lions out.

Jim Pittman
former Tulane head coach,
before facing the No. 2-ranked Vols
on Homecoming Day in Knoxville in 1967

On Game Day, I'd never really seen that kind of enthusiasm with the fans. And of course, over the years it's just gotten bigger and better. Our "107" are the best in the world. One-hundred-seven thousand. They can keep putting seats wherever they want. We still have the best fans.

Condredge Holloway
Vols star quarterback (1972-74),
All-SEC (1973)

Here, where the hills are high, Tennessee is calling on its Volunteers to give the state its first clear claim to national honors. Knoxville today is a perfect example of civil lunacy. Every suburb is a wing of an asylum.

Henry McLemore
United Press International
October 31, 1939

To play for Tennessee, you've got to get wet all over.

Leonard Coffman
fullback (1937-39)

Eugene Tucker McEver…would have been a tremendous star on any campus, and for any coach — a natural-born athlete, equipped with a perfect physique and the instinctive touch, who is generally considered to be the greatest football player ever to compete under the Orange and White banner.

Tom Siler
author and columnist, Knoxville News-Sentinel

Chapter 5

The Players

Walker Leach (1905-08) was a great halfback who I think could have made any team we have ever had at the University. He was a fine runner and a terrific kicker, both punter and place kicker. He didn't pass much, because we didn't have the halfback pass play in common use...

Nathan Dougherty

Nathan Dougherty at guard was a tower of strength, and an all-Southern man by every pick. He had well earned the leadership of the squad of the 1909, and no doubt will carry them through the season triumphantly.

Volunteer
UT yearbook

In taking Graham Vowell, captain of Tennessee, for one end we can hardly make a mistake. This chap is very big for an end, weighing 190 pounds, very fast and strong and willing. He knows the game as few ends get to know it in the South....He gets down the field like an express train, he runs hard and well with the ball, he dams things up on the defense all the time, and he catches most anything in the shape of a forward pass.

John Heisman
on naming Vowell to his 1916 all-Southern team.

Gene McEver was the greatest player I ever coached.

Gen. Robert R. Neyland

Nobody was as good as Gene McEver. He was the greatest. It's hard to compare pro players with college players, but I'm convinced that if Gene hadn't hurt his knee after his junior season at UT he would have been one of the great pro players. I played with Bronko Nagurski with the Bears, and he was probably the most powerful man I ever saw...but he couldn't break a game open like Gene could.

Beattie Feathers
all-time UT running back (1931-33)

Beattie was as good a tailback as I ever ran across.

Johnny "Hurry" Cain
star Alabama tailback

Part Indian and perhaps part antelope. A remarkable broken field runner. Want a punter? Here's your man!

Bud Fields
Bob Bertucci
on Vol great Beattie Feathers

Built like an old-time safe, but fast as a halfback.

Henry McLemore
United Press International,
Dec. 6, 1931,
on all-time Vols guard Herman Hickman

The most famous lineman in southern football in the 1930s was Tennessee's Herman Hickman. At 225 pounds, he could outrun anybody on the squad, except one or two of the fastest backs. His speed, agility, and squat power made the end and tackle on his side of the line seem superfluous.

John D. McCallum
author

Herman Hickman could demolish one side of an enemy line all by himself. He had Samson-like strength and was surprisingly nimble for all his heft.

George Trevor
New York Sun

Tennessee's so-called triple threat tailbacks were usually compared or measured by George Cafego's performance....He'll be remembered for his savage play in the 1939 Orange Bowl, which many sports writers called the most brutal game ever witnessed (Tenn. 17, Okla. 0).

Bud Fields
Bob Bertucci
authors

George Cafego is the only practice bum I've ever coached who is a genuine All-America. In practice, he can't do anything right, but for two hours on Saturdays he does everything an All-America is supposed to do.

Gen. Robert R. Neyland

For all-around brilliance, I would have to give the edge to George Cafego. But for the offense alone, Hank Lauricella is tops of my tailbacks.

Gen. Robert R. Neyland
on the best players he ever coached

He was the kind of runner who could stop on a dime, give you nine cents in change and resume along his way to the end zone.

Ed Cifers, end *(1938-40)*,
on late '30s star running back Johnny Butler

Suff had the quickest and most powerful defensive charge of any lineman I've ever seen. I have never seen a lineman play his position so well. He never made a bad play.

Gen. Robert R. Neyland
on all-time All-America guard Bob Suffridge (1938-40)

Over the years the greatest lineman we have had probably was Bob Suffridge. He was strong and fast and rugged and mean. In the backfield we've had some great ones— Gene McEver and Beattie Feathers are two of them. I've always tossed up one against the other. Feathers could be going full speed after two paces....He could get that ball and he was gone. And Gene was such a powerful runner.

Nathan Dougherty

The toughest mortal you've ever seen. He played the game like a man.

Ike Peel, UT fullback *(1939-41)*,
on Vol fullback-linebacker Len Coffman

The triple-threat Tennessee tailback is an eyeful, all right. An eyeful of wonderment, admiration, and appreciation. He can do everything. He runs, he passes, and punts with authority and artistry. A senior, Hank Lauricella is a speedy, change-of-pace runner who makes crafty use of his interference. He also…is a coffin-corner specialist, the best I've seen since Harry Kipke of Michigan.

Joe Williams
New York World-Telegram,
Nov. 4, 1951

It's true Bert can outkick Hank by five yards. But, would you rather have Bert Rechichar blocking an onrushing tackle or Hank Lauricella?

Gen. Robert R. Neyland
on his seldom use of multi-talented end Bert Rechichar
as punter or placekicker for the Vols.
Rechichar, for 17 years, held the NFL record for longest
field goal (56 yards), as a member of the Baltimore Colts,
set in a game against the Chicago Bears on Sept. 27, 1953

Johnny Majors is the equal to one of our coaches being on the field.

Bowden Wyatt
UT head coach (1955-62)

In a close ball game, a player like Johnny Majors becomes more and more valuable. He can do too many things to win a game.

Anonymous coach
at 1957 Sugar Bowl

Johnny Majors was totally unspoiled. His dad had disciplined him to listen, learn, and to work to improve. He wanted to be the best football player around, and he was willing to do whatever was necessary to reach that goal.

Harvey Robinson
UT head coach (1953-54)

The legacy of the Swamp Rat was not that Dewey Warren or any other quarterback single-handedly beat Alabama, but that he did everything necessary to see that Tennessee was successful, even if that was just holding for extra points and a field goal.

Chris Cawood
author

When you lose people like that, you've got to play a lot of defense.

Doug Dickey
UT head coach (1964-69),
on life without 1967 Vol stars
quarterback Dewey Warren,
tailback Charlie Fulton,
and All-America center Bob Johnson

Richmond Flowers was one of the fastest people in the world at that time. He had incredible speed.

Bubba Wyche
UT quarterback (1967-68)

"Look, man, you can't redshirt. We'll put you at tailback." That kind of excited him about playing tailback. So he came back out....He could run faster than anyone on the option.... I'll bet if we hadn't gotten Richmond Flowers back in 1968, we wouldn't have won six games.

> *Bill Battle*
> *UT receivers coach in 1968*

It's hard to see how any college runner could be better than Curt Watson.

> *Bill Battle*
> *1970*

Kell is the hub in an offensive line made up of dedicated athletes....Other members of the interior five rank in dependability with Kell, although none possesses Chip's unbelievable strength.

> *Bill Battle*

Bobby Majors has that genius for coming up with the play you have to have in a tight spot. He's a tremendous football player.

> *Bill Battle*
> *1971*

There wasn't a tougher guy around. There wasn't anybody who wanted to play and succeed more than Haskel Stanback. He took me under his wing when I came to UT as a 16-year-old freshman. I owe him a great deal for my success.

Condredge Holloway

Haskel Stanback has unusual ability. He is an exciting player who can come up with the big play. He is also probably the best receiver we have had in the backfield in some time.

Bill Battle
1971

I've never coached a better defensive back, and I don't know if any school has ever had one better. Roland James has it all….He's the best.

Johnny Majors
1979

I think Reggie White could become the finest defensive lineman I've ever coached before he leaves Tennessee. He should become an outstanding player....He just needs to become tougher and more aggressive.

Johnny Majors
1982

There won't be anyway to estimate what Reggie meant to us....It's inestimable. He provided, humor, leadership, morale.

Johnny Majors
on the graduation loss of Reggie White,
1984

He's one of the best I've ever seen at not wasting motion. A lot of runners give you three or four wiggles and do the two-step. Johnnie Jones just gives one wiggle and heads for the goal. It's all north and south with him.

Johnny Majors

Tony Robinson is the most dynamic college quarterback in the game since Joe Namath.

Johnny Majors

He's done it all. Didn't he get the Most Valuable Player Award? What else can you say? Fantastic. That's the word for the guy.

Johnny Majors
on 1986 Sugar Bowl MVP, quarterback Daryl Dickey

I have never known anybody in my entire association with athletics to whom it meant more to play for his school than it does for Dale Jones to play for Tennessee. He personifies what college football is all about to the highest degree.

Johnny Majors

After televising nearly 100 football games in every major conference, I've never seen a player make so many plays so consistently as Dale Jones.

Bob Neal
TBS sportscaster, 1986

Howard A. Ijams was the first UT quarterback. He played from 1891-93, a hundred years before Heath Shuler.

Chris Cawood
author

Peyton Manning is such a Tennessee icon that there's a wax statue of him in the Vols' indoor football complex and a street near the stadium is named after him.

Tim Layden
writer

I think the switch from Peyton Manning to Tee Martin has made Tennessee tougher, because they've had to build up their offensive line and rushing game.

Woody Widenhofer
Vanderbilt head coach, 1998

Tee Martin is more dangerous than Peyton Manning. He scrambles and creates another person out there who you have to be aware of.

Ainsley Battles
Vanderbilt Commodores safety

I was like this great big sponge while Peyton was here. I tried to soak up all the knowledge I could.

Tee Martin
quarterback, 1998 national champion Vols

Jamal Lewis's performance (against Syracuse) gave hope to Tennessee fans that with an improved Tee Martin at quarterback, they could have college football's most entertaining Lewis and Martin tandem since 1951, when Jerry and Dean starred in the Hollywood pigskin farce *That's My Boy.*

Ivan Maisel
writer,
1998

I don't know if we've ever had a fullback with his speed. His athleticism brings a whole new dimension.

Randy Sanders
on Shawn Bryson (1995-98; Capt. '98)

In sports I felt I had to prove myself because of my name. They say your name doesn't make a difference, but it really does.

Peerless Price
Vols' big-play wide receiver (1995-98)

From his linebacker spot, Al Wilson forced three of Florida's four fumbles with tackles of a running back at the line of scrimmage, a wide receiver in the open field and a quarterback in the pocket — a hat trick of mayhem.

Tim Layden
1998

Wilson at times was as dominant as any of the most splendid linebackers in Tennessee history, a group that includes Jack Reynolds, Steve Kiner and Keith DeLong.

Lars Anderson
writer

He's the most incredible football player I've ever seen. I'd give anything to have that kind of leadership.

Watson Brown
UAB coach

I'll do anything to win a football game.

Al Wilson
linebacker (1995-98, Capt. '98),
All-America (1998)

The Tennessee Vols All-Time Team

Offense

Wide Receiver	**Larry Seivers**
Tight End	**Bert Rechichar**
Tackle	**Dick Huffman**
Guard	**Bob Suffridge**
Center	**Bob Johnson**
Guard	**Herman Hickman**
Tackle	**Antone Davis**
Wide Receiver	**Richmond Flowers**
Quarterback	**Peyton Manning**
Running Back	**Johnny Majors**
Running Back	**Beattie Feathers**

Defense

Defensive End	**Doug Atkins**
Defensive Tackle	**Reggie White**
Nose Guard/Tackle	**Steve DeLong**
Defensive End	**Leonard Little**
Linebacker	**Steve Kiner**
Linebacker	**Frank Emanuel**
Linebacker	**Jack Reynolds**
Cornerback	**Dale Carter**
Safety	**Bobby Majors**
Safety	**Bobby Dodd**
Cornerback	**Roland James**
Punter	**Ron Widby**
Kicker	**Fuad Reveiz**
Kick Returner	**Willie Gault**
Coach	**Gen. Robert Neyland**

Captain Neyland is an excellent prospect as a coach. He is a maker of ends.

John J. McEwan
head coach, Army,
1925

The best move I ever made.

Dean Nathan Dougherty
on the hiring of Robert Neyland
as a coach for the Tennessee Vols,
1925 (first hired as an assistant coach)

Chapter 6

The Coaches

Until J.A. Pierce showed up on campus in 1899 as the first full-time coach hired by the Athletic Association, the coaching chores had been divided among students, faculty members, players, and YMCA officials. These were the days when coaches would appear for a season or two and then be just as quickly gone. Pierce, a graduate of LaFayette, lasted two seasons, 1899 and 1900, but he departed with an admirable record: eight wins, four losses, and a tie.

Russ Bebb
author, The Big Orange

The coaches of our day would undertake to give us rules on training so as to get us in some physical condition. He coached all the players in how to play their positions and, as a matter of fact, as a player I had to learn on my own. The coach didn't know how to play guard; he was an end. So you just learned after a year or two how to play guard. You had the advantage over the other fellow who hadn't had the experience.

Nathan Dougherty

Zora Clevenger has developed teams that are strikingly in contrast to those of the last two or three seasons. He has formulated plans for even greater improvements next year, and the very character of the man proves that these plans will be carried out.

Volunteer
1912

Coach Banks came along too early. I was always impressed with him as an offensive coach and as a man. He was a genius when it came to offense, but when it came to defense he was totally lacking. If Coach Banks had come along in this day and age when you have offensive and defensive coaches, he would have been ranked with the great ones on offense.

J.G. Lowe
end (1922-25; Capt. 1924, '25)

Tennessee fans can look forward to a team which will display a world of fight every minute on the field. The attitude of the players indicates opponents will spend one long day in the brief sixty minutes they face the Vols.

Capt. Robert R. Neyland
two days before the start of practice
in his first year as Tennessee head coach, 1926.

The General

Behind an attacking single-wing offense, a smothering 6-2-2-1 defense, and characteristic military-style precision and discipline gained while a cadet at West Point, General Robert Reese Neyland guided the Tennessee Volunteers from 1926-52 to the heights of college football supremacy.

Neyland coached 21 seasons over a 27-year span (active military service interrupted his tenure during the 1935 season and from 1941-45). In over two decades as head coach, Neyland toppled arch rival Vanderbilt 16 times with only three losses. Two were ties. Up till the time Neyland came on board, the Vols had won just two of 21 meetings with Vandy. Overall, the General went on to register 173 career wins at Tennessee, while losing just 31 games and tying 12.

Neyland Novelties

In addition to being the inventor of tearaway jerseys, six-man defensive lines, and low-cut shoes, General Neyland is credited with being the first in the South to install telephones linking the pressbox roof and sideline bench; the first to utilize lighter hip pads; the first to employ a cover over the field; and the first to house his players in motels instead of hotels.

We should make use of the quick kick. The only defense for a good quick kick is to know how to return one.

Gen. Robert R. Neyland

A poorly designed play well executed is much better than a well-designed play poorly executed.

Gen. Robert R. Neyland

You don't develop good teeth by eating mush. You don't keep a blocker sharp by giving him theory and letting him go through the motions in practice.

Gen. Robert R. Neyland

A man can live without love but not without work.

Gen. Robert R. Neyland

One interferer is worth three ball carriers.

Gen. Robert R. Neyland

Gentlemen, touchdowns follow blocking as sure as night follows day.

Gen. Robert R. Neyland

Neyland is the greatest coach in the country. He teaches blocking and tackling, and after all, that *is* football.

Lynn Bomar
Vanderbilt Commodore end/halfback (1921-24),
Dec. 9, 1939

Naturally, I am prejudiced, because I played for him, but I believe that the General was the greatest coach ever to come out of the South. If you doubt me, go back and read his record over again: 173 wins, 31 losses, and 12 ties for a 27-year record, with time out for war and military service. He placed the Volunteers in seven bowl games, made the Neyland system of play the most respected in football, and founded a genuine dynasty of college football coaches unparalleled in modern gridiron history.

Herman Hickman
all-time UT guard (1929-31), All-America (1931),
and longtime Yale University head coach

General Robert Neyland has had more influence on college football in the last 30 years than any other man. He believed in the elastic defense. He'd let you catch a short pass for 6 or 8 yards but no long TD passes....Coach Neyland believed more in ball position than ball control. Those of us who learned under him rely on position. We'd rather let you have the ball on your own 10 than take it ourselves on our 30. Eventually you're going to make a mistake.

> *Bobby Dodd*
> *star quarterback and all-time UT safety (1928-30),*
> *legendary Georgia Tech head coach,*
> *1959*

He emphasized the alert defensive frame of mind as no other coach I've known.

> *Fred Russell*
> *Nashville Banner,*
> *on Gen. Robert Neyland*

Neyland somehow managed to reduce a complex game down to its simplest basics.

> *Ben Byrd*
> *sports editor, Knoxville New-Sentinel*

The more sophisticated breed of college athlete today would split a gut laughing at one of those "up-and-at-'em" fight talks, but Herman Hickman was able to sprout poetry without provoking snickers. Grantland Rice, his fellow Tennessean, labeled him the Poet Laureate of the Great Smokies. Before a Harvard-Yale game, stout Herman rallied his Eli troops by reciting Patrick Henry's Revolutionary War speech: "I can hear the chains clanking in the streets of Boston; the Redcoats are forging them for you."

John D. McCallum

Good defense is getting
11 men around the ball
with all of them in a nasty
mood.

Bowden Wyatt

I believe the University of Tennessee head football job is the best coaching job in the country.

Doug Dickey
1969

I'm a Tennessean.

Bill Battle
former UT head coach and star end
at Alabama (1960-62), when asked
if he were an Alabaman or Alabamian

A winning coach will learn through proper channels the thinking of his players. This becomes an important part in the motivation of a player and team.

Bill Battle

In my opinion, Bill Battle never received the recognition to which he was entitled.

Bear Bryant

You could tell then that Johnny (Majors) had a great coaching future ahead of him. He had been schooled in the fundamentals of the game by his father, and then he had learned even more while playing at Tennessee. He was a solid, enthusiastic assistant coach.

> *Frank Broyles*
> *longtime Arkansas head coach,*
> *on whose staff Majors served*
> *as an assistant (1964-67)*

I've made my share of mistakes but the biggest one was not getting the right people together on my coaching staff sooner.

> *Johnny Majors*

Coach Cafego has probably been the most influential person that I've ever met, in terms of getting something done. He's like a father to all the kickers.

> *Fuad Reveiz*
> *UT kicker (1981-84)*

I don't think there is anybody who knows more about kicking than George Cafego.

> *Bill Battle*

Recruit good players, coach them hard with discipline, and win football games. That's what we've done. It's worked.

Phillip Fulmer

Offensive linemen are the most detailed of players. We tend to be solid citizens, well-organized by necessity, lesser athletes who have to work harder. We take more punishment than we give out and take it stoically. When we have a great game, the quarterback and the running back get the credit. Phillip embodies all of that.

Bill Curry
*former NFL All-Pro center and
head coach at Georgia Tech, Alabama and Kentucky,
on Vols head coach Phil Fulmer*

Do you get the feeling that Robert Reese Neyland would laugh if he saw what college football has become? Or maybe cry? What would he think of seeing grown men dance like chickens after a touchdown? How would he feel about drawing up a defensive strategy against somebody's four-wideout set for the Insight.com Bowl, then being interviewed by Dr. Jerry Punch on the ESPN postgame show while Gatorade was dumped on him by his players and Jay-Z's *Hard Knock Life* blared over the stadium's loudspeakers?

Jeff Pearlman
writer

We won with TENN-icity.

Johnnie Jones
UT star running back (1982-84, Co-Capt. '84)

Chapter 7

Winning and Losing

A squad can become bloated with victory upon victory. An occasional defeat is a fine alkalizer.

Fred Russell
sports editor, Nashville Banner,
Jan. 2, 1940,
after undefeated and unscored upon
1939 Vols lost to Southern California
14–0 in the 1940 Rose Bowl

Champions don't lose happily. And Tennessee lost like champions yesterday.

F.M. Williams
Nashville Tennessean, Jan, 2, 1957,
after No. 2-ranked Vols 13–7 Sugar Bowl loss
to 11th-ranked Baylor

A truly great Southern California team won from a truly brave but unequal Tennessee team. The gallant Southerners, wave upon courageous wave, flung themselves on the lances of Troy and died horridly but very impressively.

Davis J. Walsh
Los Angeles Examiner,
Jan. 2, 1940,
after Vols 1940 Rose Bowl loss to USC

Some day a Tennessee football team may play a more rousing second half than it did in the 1968 Orange Bowl throbber, but if and when that happens, the odds are about a thousand to one it won't be a losing effort.

Fred Russell
Nashville Banner, Jan 2, 1968,
after UT's 24-point second-half comeback
against Oklahoma fell short by two points

We seniors felt a bond, I know. And we could sense that everyone was telling himself, "They're not 19 points better than we are. We can still win."

Bob Johnson
captain, 1967 Vols,
after 26–24 loss to Oklahoma in 1968 Orange Bowl.
UT had been down 19–0 at halftime.

If the Russians had a football team, maybe I'd rather beat them than Tennessee.

Chuck Fairbanks
Oklahoma head coach,
after the Sooners narrow 1968 Orange Bowl win over UT

We've had a few bad teams and some bad coaching, but the good times outnumber the bad by a lot.

Johnny Majors
Dec. 30, 1985

The infectious germ of being a winner.

Malcolm Aitken
captain, 1932 Vols,
on what he remembered most about Tennessee football

From that day on, Tennessee always brought the fourth dimension into action — the confidence bred from winning.

John D. McCallum
after UT's landmark 15–13 victory over Alabama,
October 20, 1928

If my teams win, my press will be good. If we lose, the press can't help me anyhow.

Gen. Robert R. Neyland

Avoid losing games before you try to win.

Doug Dickey

That's when Coach Dickey learned you don't sit on a lead with Coach Bryant.

Richmond Flowers
All-America wingback (1967),
on UT's 11–10 loss to Alabama in 1966,
after leading at one time 10–0

We won because we knew we were better prepared than our opponents. Coach Neyland gave us the edge.

Buddy Hackman
one of the "Flaming Sophomores,"
1928

Winning is what the game of football is all about. Hitting is the name of the game, and after all, football is a battle of individuals.

Bill Battle

All you do is tell Bubba Wyche to throw passes, Richmond Flowers to catch them, Albert Dorsey to intercept when Ken Stabler throws, and Steve Kiner to intercept Alabama's runners. And there you have it.

Doug Dickey
on how to beat Alabama (1967)

The biggest thing about winning a national championship is the knowledge that you have accomplished something that can't be taken away.

Johnny Majors

The biggest thing that caused problems for me at Tennessee was not being able to beat Alabama and Auburn regularly.

Bill Battle

I've wondered several times if I'd be remembered so easily if I'd made that field goal.

Gary "Wide" Wright
UT placekicker (1966, '67),
on missing the 19-yard field goal in the rain at Knoxville
that cost the Vols a win over Alabama in 1966

I knew we were going to win the Arkansas game. I was trying to figure out how when their quarterback dropped the ball.

Raynoch Thompson
linebacker,
on Vols' miraculous 28–24 win over undefeated Arkansas
to keep UT's 1998 national champion hopes alive.

...One of the hardest things a program has to do is break the ice against an opponent that has been on a long winning streak.

Johnny Majors

If you want your quarterback to be successful, you have to give him the opportunity on a level playing field to do that.

Condredge Holloway

Four steps back, two steps to the left, look up once at the goalpost. Then I don't think about anything, because thought clutters the routine.

Jeff Hall
kicker (1995-98),
UT's all-time leading scorer

Tennessee has won a lot of games playing defense. This was one.

Walter Slater
Vol tailback (1941, '42, '46 (Capt.),
after UT's 1943 Sugar Bowl win over Tulsa (14–7)

Lord, we are thankful we have gone this far. We hope each and every one of us can play this game as well as we did those of the past. We are thankful to be here and we pray we can win. Amen.

Sam Bartholomew
captain, 1939 Tennessee Volunteers,
before taking the field in the 1940 Rose Bowl

Sometimes you've just got to win ugly.

Phillip Fulmer
head coach of the 1998 national champion Vols

Legend has it that boys grow into men in the span of one afternoon whenever the Vols meet the Tide.

Ben Byrd

Chapter 8

The Rivalries

The Volunteers have fought some courageous and heartrending skirmishes in both victory and defeat since they traded coonskin caps and muskets for a prolate pigskin spheroid called a football in 1891.

Kentucky, Vanderbilt, Ole Miss, Georgia Tech, Auburn, even Sewanee…all have been fierce Vol rivals over the years, over the eras.

But though they've played against each other since 1916, it wasn't until the early 1990s that Florida and Tennessee became arch rivals. Two irritants fueled the furnace: 1) Five straight defeats from 1993 through 1997, all under Phillip Fulmer's reign. 2) That old salt-in-the-wound master himself, Steve Spurrier, Florida's brilliant if not likable coach. Maybe it was just payback time for the fact that Tennessee had swept the first ten games in the series and 13 of the first 15 contests between the two through 1971. Regardless, the duel is a hot item now.

For sheer grandeur in Southern rivalries, though, nothing comes close to Tennessee-Alabama. For a fan of the Orange and White, the blood pressure rises at the mere mention of the rancorous Tide. For the Vol nation, no bell rings more ominously and anxiously than the tolling of the Third Saturday in October.

Dixie's Finest — Alabama vs. Tennessee

For a Tennessee football player, there is no better time to be a hero than The Third Saturday in October.

> — *Mike Strange*
> *Knoxville News-Sentinel,*
> *October 20, 1985*

It has been called the biggest game in the South. Almost a century old, the Alabama-Tennessee rivalry has yielded some timeless classics. In true warrior fashion, Bear Bryant played in the 1935 game (Alabama, 25–0) with a broken leg. In another era, UT defensive back Albert Dorsey virtually assured All-America selection when, in 1967, he intercepted three passes in the Alabama game.

In the 1966 contest, Tennessee surrendered a 10-point lead in the rain at Knoxville, falling behind 11–10 before the Vols' Gary "Wide" Wright missed a game-winning field goal from the 19 in the closing seconds. It was a bitter loss for Tennessee and UT fans. Tide celebrants said Bear Bryant left Knoxville that day "walking on water." That game more than any other fueled the fire in the modern era between the two interstate and conference rivals.

Unruly Tie Opens Alabama Rivalry

With argumentative spectators bursting onto the field after virtually every down, Tennessee and Alabama kicked off their storied rivalry on November 28, 1901, in Birmingham, with a 6–6 tie.

The *Birmingham News* reported the following day in its account of the game, "The combined efforts of a squad of policemen, assisted by a number of citizens, were of little avail against the curiosity of the majority of the enthusiasts who, forgetful of everything but that the game was in progress, rushed at will upon the gridiron, forcing officials to call time until the players could secure more room."

That fall, 1902, we had a terrific football game with Vanderbilt (Vanderbilt 12, Tennessee 5 — October 25, 1902). I got loose for a long run, no one t'wixt me and the goal line except Vandy quarterback Frank Kyle, an Old Fox and a good 'un too. We didn't know about, or have, the downfield blocking for which the Vols are famous nowadays. So, in desperation, I tried hard, but unsuccessfully, to hurdle Kyle. Sitting there disconsolate in defeat that could have been victory, I realized to the fullest how...thrills can be two-edged....Oh, death where is thy sting.

Theophilus Nash Buckingham
UT fullback and offensive tackle, (1901, '02; Capt. '02)

It may be a long way to Tipperary, but the longest roads end somewhere. For 20 years Tennessee football teams have been trying to accomplish what many thought was the impossible; for 20 years Volunteer teams have been marching up the hill, only to turn around and march right down again, but today, they pulled the hill down with them.

Knoxville Sentinel
Nov. 8, 1914,
after Tennessee's monumental 16–14 victory over Vanderbilt
— its first victory ever over VU in 13 meetings

The 1923 Float Bowl vs. Kentucky

Like Vanderbilt in the early years of the twenti-eth century, Kentucky gave Tennessee all they could handle, taking 10 of the first 15 games in the series against the Volunteers.

The 1923 game, an 18–0 Tennessee victory, was an instant classic, played in a driving, freezing rain.

Before the contest in Lexington, Vols coach M.B. Banks sent his team manager to the field to report on the mud. His evaluation: "There is no mud, but half the field is covered with water."

During a scoreless first half, the UT punter had to kick from the end zone several times. Each time he failed to get the ball beyond the 10-yard line.

"The water was so deep on the field that the football actually floated at times," recalled two-time Tennessee captain J.G. Lowe. "The referee would have to move the ball to other spots along the line. At halftime we got in the showers and cleaned our uniforms and bodies."

The Vols finally scored late in the fourth quar-ter. Ahead 6–0, UT kicked off, deliberately booting it on the ground. The ball floated into the end zone, where UT recovered for its second touchdown. "The same thing happened on the next kickoff," said Lowe, "and in three plays we had scored 18 points."

1949 Vols Make Most of Vandy Turnovers

In the 43rd meeting between the two Volunteer State rivals, at Shields-Watkins Field in 1949, Tennessee, behind excellent defensive and special teams play, built a 13–0 lead on an interception return and a blocked punt, both for scores.

Sophomore tailback Hank Lauricella's pass to Bert Rechichar made it 19–0 Vols in the second period. Then, incredibly, UT gave up 20 second-quarter points to Vandy to head, stunned, to the locker room, one point down at the half.

But the Vols caught a break early in the third period. Vandy's Lee Nalley, brushed by Tennessee's Chaddie Baker just before fielding Lauricella's high punt, fumbled and the Vols recovered. UT converted the turnover into a score, then watched the Commodores self-destruct by throwing an interception and fumbling three times in the time remaining.

Statistically, Vanderbilt recorded 18 first downs to just two for Tennessee and amassed 354 total yards to UT's paltry 111. But the Vols capitalized on the plethora of turnovers to make the difference in the 26–20 final score.

The Recruitment of Richmond Flowers

Another element provoking interstate hostility and tension between Tennessee and Alabama was Tennessee's celebrated recruitment of All-America prep running back and high hurdler Richmond Flowers. Flowers, the son of the Alabama state attorney general, was the top recruiting prospect in America in 1964. It was almost state law back then that any Alabama blue-chip high school ace automatically would fall into the fold of the deistic Bear Bryant. But Flowers' father, a ranking Democrat with a reputation for being a moderate on the hot civil rights issues of the times, had been the target of pro-segregationists within the state and eventually was ousted from his powerful position. After the series of upsetting events leading up to his father's leave of office, Richmond Flowers Jr. signed a national letter-of-intent with Tennessee. A statewide furor erupted in Alabama, when it was announced that the schoolboy star had turned his back on The Bear and was headed to Knoxville.

Alabamians gloated when Flowers, who had emerged as a sophomore star wingback for the Big Orange, and his teammates were the victims of a humiliating 11–10 loss in 1966 in the mud at Shields-Watkins Field, in the Alabama native's debut against his homestate icon.

But the talented Flowers would get his sweet revenge. The following year, in 1967, at Birmingham's Legion Field, UT crushed the Tide 24–13. Shifted to tailback his senior season, in 1968, Flowers' over-the-top touchdown leap gave Tennessee a payback (for 1966) 10–9 win in Knoxville.

The Vols star was also a world-class high hurdler while on The Hill. One-tenth of a second was all that separated Flowers from owning the world records in the 60-yard dash, 60-yard high hurdles, and the outdoor 120-yard high hurdles. Sadly, in 1968, his senior season, a hamstring injury killed his hopes of an Olympic gold medal in his specialty, the high hurdles — a year in which he had been running undefeated.

But Flowers moved on as a second-round selection of the Dallas Cowboys in the 1969 NFL draft. Switched to a defensive back in the pros, he spent two and a half years with Dallas before being traded to the New York Giants, where he finished out his career (through 1973).

You have to believe you can beat Alabama. No one ever believed they could beat them till that day (Oct. 15, 1966 — Tennessee's 11–10 loss to Alabama). We moved on them at will, sat on the lead, then moved back at will. We knew we were a better football team and Alabama knew we were a better football team.

Richmond Flowers

We were there to beat them, and we *knew* we could beat them.

Richmond Flowers
on playing Alabama at Legion Field in 1967,
the year after UT's attitude-changing
11–10 loss in the rain to the Tide in Knoxville.
The '67 Vols rolled up a decisive 24–13 win.

Someday, Johnnie, you're going to score the winning touchdown against Alabama.

Ed Murphey
UT fan instrumental in recruiting Johnnie Jones.
Murphey's prediction came true: Jones' 66-yard
fourth-quarter TD run gave the Vols a 41–34 win
over the Tide in 1983.

We all remember the things we do in the Alabama game.

Johnny Majors

I think if God wants something to happen, it's going to happen. I won't give luck the credit. I give the credit to God. He's standing up there right now, with Smokey next to him, wearing an orange jersey.

Tee Martin
on the miraculous last-minute win over Arkansas
to keep UT unbeaten and top-ranked in 1998

Chapter 9

Great Moments

He could do everything
a football player should do,
and when it came to kicking
a football, he was in a class
to himself. Toots Douglas was
an All-American football player.

Raymond Harris

Longest Punt in UT History Set in 1902

Neither UT career punting leader Jimmy Colquitt, nor Craig Colquitt, nor Neil Clabo, nor Hank Lauricella, nor Ron Widby, nor Herman "Thunderfoot" Weaver...none of these great Vol punters hold the UT record for longest punt.

That distinguished mark is in the possession of an old-timer, set just 12 years after the birth of football on the UT campus.

Only one week following the big win at Georgia Tech in 1902, the University of Tennessee record book added a listing that has never been topped in the well-over 100 years of Big Orange football.

Hugh "Toots" Douglas, playing at old Baldwin Park on a field that was 110 yards long, rocketed a gargantuan 100-yard punt in an 11–0 loss to Clemson and its legendary coach John Heisman, on November 27, 1902.

Called by Heisman the longest kick he ever saw, the *Knoxville Journal* carried this account of the record punt.

"Douglas...dropped a kick for an even 100 yards, the sphere sailing from Tennessee's 5-yard line, where Clemson had carried it, to Clemson's 20-yard line, from which it bounded to the 5-yard line and was caught by Henvey."

McEver's 98-Yard Opening Kickoff Return Against Alabama Ushered in New Era for Vols

The most brilliant of Tennessee's "Flaming Sophomores" of 1928, Gene McEver gained Volunteer immortality for his 98-yard opening kickoff return for a touchdown against Alabama on October 20, 1928.

McEver, in the dressing room before the game, clairvoyantly told his teammates, "If I get that ball on the kickoff everybody try to cut down a man; if you can't cut down a man, just move over and let me through."

Then in his own words McEver describes what happened minutes later on the field:

"After our guys put nine of theirs on the ground, I saw those two Alabama players up there in 'the alley' about midfield. I went right between 'em, split 'em. I just bowed my neck and let 'em have it. That's all I could do. I don't know to this day whether anybody chased me to the goal."

The legendary score ignited UT to an undefeated season and, some say, brought the Vols into the limelight of national respectability for the first time. McEver, Tennessee's first genuine All-America, still ranks as the Vols' all-time career leader in touchdowns, with 44.

I had the pleasure of being on the first two teams to defeat Vanderbilt (1914, '16) and to lick Sewanee and Alabama.

Graham "Little" Vowel
(1914, '15, '16; Capt. '21)

That punt return by Red Harp for 82 yards in the last two minutes to beat a fine Duke team (15–13 in 1936) was my greatest thrill in sports.

DeWitt Weaver
(1934-36; Capt. '36)

Being a member of three straight unde-feated teams in three straight bowls (Orange, Rose, Sugar) offered enough thrills.

Norbert Ackermann
(1938, '39, '40; Capt. '40)

Faking Charlie "Choo Choo" Justice out of position on a fake lateral off a punt return was my greatest thrill.

Walter Slater
whose punt return for a TD vs. North Carolina
enabled UT to win 20–14, in 1946

Feathers-Cain Epic 1932 Punting Duel In Rain and Mud

*Feathers' keg-calved right leg hung
them high and deep.*
— *1983 UT Media Guide*

The Tennessee-Alabama game of 1932 featured what many observers feel was the best punting duel of all time in college football history.

Tennessee's magnificent part Indian-part antelope tailback, Beattie Feathers, squared off against the Tide's sensational Johnny "Hurry" Cain, described by Feathers as the best player he ever played against. The two giant stars kicked a water-soaked ball back and forth all afternoon on mud-caked Legion Field in Birmingham. Incredibly, Feathers booted 23 times for a 46-yard average, while Cain posted a 43-yard average on 19 punts.

For most of the contest, it looked like Alabama's first-half field goal was going to hold up. But Tennessee's magnificent analytical strategist, Coach Robert Neyland, saw to it that UT got the wind in the fourth quarter. With the breeze to his back, Feathers unleashed a boot that rolled dead on the Alabama one. Cain, on first down and under tremendous pressure, shanked his punt and watched it die at the Tide 12, his only bad kick of the game. Three plays later, Feathers scored to make it a 7–3 final in favor of Tennessee.

Old George (Cafego) really laid the wood to that All-American end, Waddy Young (Oklahoma). That was a solid legal lick in what was to be the roughest, toughest physical contact football game I ever played or saw. It almost turned into a brawl several times.

Bowden Wyatt
UT captain (1938) and Vols head coach (1955-62),
on the 1939 Orange Bowl victory over Oklahoma (17–0),
in which Wyatt kicked a field goal

I'd probably have to say my most thrilling hour came in the 1943 Sugar Bowl when I blocked a Glenn Dobbs' punt for a safety.

Denver Crawford
(1942, '46, '47; Capt. '47),
better known for his devastating block
that took out three Vanderbilt Commodores
on Hal Littleford's punt return for a touchdown
that beat Vandy 14–6 in 1947.

Personally, my greatest thrill at Tennessee was watching our 1967 team gathering itself after losing to UCLA in the opener and build a head of steam that lasted for nine games.

Bob Johnson

Johnny Butler was the whole show in 1939...That was the greatest run I ever saw. He went 56 yards from scrimmage, but I guess Johnny must have scampered around 200 yards dodging people. Not a single Alabama player managed to lay a hand on him.

Bob Suffridge

$2,500 a yard.
$833 a foot.
$72 an inch.
That is what Johnny Butler's touchdown run against Auburn's Tigers on Saturday was worth to the University of Tennessee. It means the Rose Bowl, and that flower-scented extravaganza carries a reward of $100,000.

Henry McLemore
United Press International
Dec. 12, 1939

That was a pretty tough run for a sophomore back to make. He had the weight of the Bowl on his shoulders and a bouquet of roses in his arms.

Henry McLemore

Butler's TD Dashes Ensure Unscored Upon '39 Season

Having become an overnight star earlier in the 1939 season when he reeled off a 56-yard broken-field touchdown run to stun Alabama, second-string tailback Johnny Butler, "Mercury in a head-gear" according to United Press writer Henry McLemore, saved the Vols' unbeaten and unscored-upon regular season by ripping off another spectacular long scoring run — a 40-yarder — in the regular season finale, a 7–0 victory against Auburn, to send Tennessee to the Rose Bowl.

Butler's 56-yarder against the Tide is considered by longtime UT observers to be the most spectacular broken field run ever witnessed on Shields-Watkins Field. Three times the "swivel-hipped" Butler reversed his field on the serpentine run behind perfectly executed downfield blocking — a Vols' trademark under General Neyland.

Quick Kicks Highlight Battle of Unbeatens in '56

The *Knoxville News-Sentinel*'s Tom Siler, a respected authority on southern football, called it "one of the classics of fundamental football."

In 1956, Tennessee, ranked No. 3 in the nation, and Georgia Tech, No. 2 behind a juggernaut Oklahoma Sooner team on its way to its third straight undefeated season, met on November 3rd at Neyland Stadium, both unbeaten and untied.

"It was a fiery duel of inspired defensive play and unforgettable kicking," recalled Siler.

After Tech was stopped early in the game and punted to the Tennessee 6-yard line, UT All-America tailback Johnny Majors ripped off a 16-yard gain, before surprising the Yellow Jackets with a 68-yard quick kick to the Tech 10-yard line. The game became a study in tactics with tremendous defense and astounding punting. Another Majors' punt stopped dead at the Tech one-inch line. Substitute Vols tailback Bobby Gordon rocketed a 72-yarder later in the game. It was scoreless at the half.

The game's only score came in the third period, when Tennessee All-America end Buddy Cruze got behind Tech's Paul Rotenberry and corralled a Majors' pass for 45 yards to the 1. On the next play fullback Tommy Bronson plunged over. Final score: Tennessee 6, Georgia Tech 0. The Vols went on to finish the regular season undefeated.

I've been told that my best game was against Georgia Tech in 1957, but I don't remember much about it. I caught a pass for a first down at Tech's one...I was out cold. They say I kept playing and later ran the reverse for about 40 yards and a touchdown. I was taking a shower after the game when I finally came to and I had to ask the score.

Bill Anderson
Vol end (1955-57; Co-Capt. '57),
and longtime color analyst for John Ward on UT broadcasts

My greatest thrill at UT? It may very well have been my senior year when I scored that over-the-top touchdown (against Alabama) that allowed us to beat them 10–9, when *they* were a better team. They went down and missed a chip-shot field goal themselves (referring to UT's last-second loss to Alabama on a missed field goal during Flowers' sophomore season. See page 87).

Richmond Flowers

Vols Silence Cannon, End LSU's Repeat Title Bid

In quest of back-to-back national championships, LSU and its All-America halfback Billy Cannon came to Knoxville on Nov. 7, 1959, riding the nation's longest winning streak, at 19 games.

Though the great Bayou Bengal express crunched out 334 total yards to Tennessee's mere 112, the Tigers were down 14–7 in the final quarter, thanks to an interception return for a touchdown by Vol cornerback Jim Cartwright and an LSU fumble that led to a second UT score. But a Tennessee bobble on its own 2-yard line in the fourth quarter brought the Tigers to within a point at 14–13. LSU coach Paul Dietzel then made a fateful call to go for two and the win. The Vols, anticipating that the great Cannon would get the ball, stuffed the soon-to-be-named Heisman Trophy winner on an off-tackle slant just 18 inches short of the goal line. Dietzel later remarked:

"We went to Knoxville to win, not to tie....It was a tough defeat...I would have loved winning the national title twice in a row."

Tennessee Turf

In the fall of 1968, Tennessee unveiled a new look in football in the South. In lieu of Bermuda, bent grass, rye and a touch of crabgrass, Vols football was being played for the first time on an artificial surface called Tartan Turf. The infamous revolutionary rug had made its way onto the collegiate fields of play.

Interestingly, some UT opponents thought that it was a decided home-field "psychological" advantage for the Vols. Regardless, the inaugural game — the 1968 season opener against Georgia — was a classic.

With the Bulldogs holding a seemingly secure 17–9 lead late in the game, Tennessee had come down to its final possession. Starting at their own 20, the Vols began their climactic march downfield. The drive appeared to stall on the Georgia 20, where UT faced a critical fourth-down situation. Time for only one more play remained. Clutch quarterback Bubba Wyche then calmly stepped up and delivered a 20-yard scoring toss to Gary Kreis that pulled the Vols to within two. Time had already expired when Tennessee lined up for the two-point conversion attempt. Again Wyche came through, connecting with Ken DeLong to close out the "artificial" thriller at 17–17.

Vols Claw Back from Greatest Deficit, Beat Notre Dame

Down a deflating 31–7 just before halftime, Tennessee's 1991 Vols accomplished something no other opponent in Notre Dame's imposing football history had ever done — climb back from 24 points behind to defeat the Irish at Notre Dame.

With the stigma of utter humiliation resting squarely on their collective shoulders, the Volunteers regrouped just before halftime on a Darryl Hardy block of a Craig Hentrich field goal attempt. UT's Floyd Miley recovered the ball and returned it 85 yards for a touchdown. Still, Tennessee trailed 31–14 at the half.

UT quarterback Andy Kelly quickly got the Vols moving in the third period with a TD pass to Von Reeves, but Tennessee still needed two TDs to win. This was no pushover Notre Dame squad. The Irish featured a devastating running back tandem of Jerome Bettis and Reggie Brooks and the Joe Montana-like wizardry of Rick Mirer at quarterback, not to mention the gifted toe of Hentrich, a future Pro Bowler with the NFL's Tennessee Oilers.

In the final quarter, Aaron Hayden, the Vols' leading rusher on the day (82 yards), stepped up with a pair of touchdowns, after a final Irish three-pointer from Hentrich, to complete the greatest comeback in Tennessee history, 35–34.

It was like shooting darts
and hitting the bull's-eye.

Tee Martin
on his NCAA record-setting passing performance
at South Carolina (Oct. 31, 1998),
where he connected on 23 consecutive passes
for a 95.8 completion percentage.
His achievement broke Kent Austin's 16-year-old
SEC mark of 20. By the second quarter, Martin had sur-
passed Peyton Manning's UT standard of 12 straight passes.

God bless the guy who dropped it. Let me
know I'm not perfect. Keep on working hard.

Tee Martin
on UT wideout David Martin's drop of his 24th and final pass
against South Carolina, denying him a perfect 24-for-24.

I wouldn't call it a miracle. How about... dramatic?

Phillip Fulmer
on Tennessee's deus-ex-machina 28–24 win
over Arkansas in 1998
to keep national title hopes alive

Other Great Big Orange Moments

- Bobby Dodd's great defensive work to beat Florida 13–12 in 1928.
- Breezy Wynn's flat-on-the-ground field goal to beat Duke, 16–13, in 1932.
- J.D. Proctor's three TD passes to Jim Powell to beat Ole Miss 18–14 in 1946.
- Bert Rechichar's SEC-record 100-yard punt return and 50-yard interception return, both for touchdowns, in a 27–20 victory over Washington & Lee in 1950.
- The Hank Lauricella-to-Bert Rechichar pass that beat Kentucky and Babe Parilli 7–0 in 1950 (Bear Bryant was then UK coach).
- Hank Lauricella's 75-yard run in the 1951 Cotton Bowl win over Texas (20–14), in which he reversed his field three times.
- Ray Martin's 100-yard TD interception return of a Johnny Unitas pass, in a 59–6 rout of Louisville in 1953.
- Sammy Burklow's field goal to win the 1957 Gator Bowl, 3–0, over Texas A&M.
- George Hunt's last-second three-pointer to beat South Carolina, 20–18 (1970).
- Fifth-year senior Jimmy Maxwell's guiding of the Vols to 9–2 season in 1971. The rags-to-riches story included a 14–13 Liberty Bowl win over Arkansas.

He reminds me of Nat Moore.
McGee's smooth like Moore and he
goes up and gets the ball in a crowd.
He's tough in the clutch. When I see
Tim McGee, I think of Nat Moore.
And when I see Nat Moore, I think of
Tim McGee.

Tolbert Bain
Miami Hurricanes cornerback,
1985

Chapter 10

Receiver U.

He has perfected different patterns instead of just trying to outrun everybody, and he has made himself a threat in front of the defender as well as behind him.

Doug Dickey
on former Vol All-America wingback Richmond Flowers

The tradition of receivers Willie Gault, Mike Miller, Darryal Wilson, Clyde Duncan and Lenny Taylor is there. I just hope I'm the next in line for some of the good things that happened to them.

Tim McGee
wide receiver (1983, '84, '85 Tri-Capt.)
All-America (1985)

Half the time he's covered, he's still going to catch it.

Steve Spurrier
1966 Heisman Trophy winner and
University of Florida head coach,
on the Vols' Carl Pickens

We're No. 1

In a seven-year span, between 1982 and 1988, five standout Vol wide receivers were selected in the first round of the annual NFL draft:

Anthony Hancock (1982, Kansas City)
Willie Gault (1983, Chicago)
Clyde Duncan (1984, St. Louis Cardinals)
Tim McGee (1986, Cincinnati)
Anthony Miller (1988, San Diego)

Other UT wide receivers who were first-round picks were **Stanley Morgan** (1977, New England), **Alvin Harper** (1991, Dallas) and **Marcus Nash** (1998, Denver).

In all, Tennessee, through the 1999 draft, has had 31 former players taken as No. 1 picks. Two ex-Vols, tailback **George Cafego** (1940, Chicago Cardinals) and quarterback **Peyton Manning** (1998, Indianapolis), were the top overall pick of their respective drafts.

Back in our era, we had one speed guy and one possession guy. Stanley Morgan was definitely our big playmaker, the guy we tried to get the ball to as much as possible.

Condredge Holloway

When there was a clutch situation that needed maybe a jump ball, where everything was equal, and you needed a guy who could go up and get the ball, that guy was Larry Seivers.

Condredge Holloway

Larry Seivers is an absolute marvel…

Bill Battle

Peerless is carrying on the tradition. He's explosive. He fits right in the mold.

Tim McGee

Peerless was always a really good receiver, but this year he's made more big plays than anybody we've had here in some time.

Phillip Fulmer
1998

The Great Ends and Wideouts at Receiver U.

Bowden Wyatt *(1936-38; Capt. '38)*
Bud Sherrod *(1947-50)*
Bert Rechichar *(1949-51; Capt. '51)*
Buddy Cruze *(1955-56)*
Johnny Mills *(1964-66)*
Richmond Flowers *(1966-68)*
Stanley Morgan *(1973-76)*
Larry Seivers *(1974-76; Co-Capt. '76)*
Anthony Hancock *(1978-81)*
Willie Gault *(1979-82)*
Mike Miller *(1980-82)*
Clyde Duncan *(1981-83)*
Tim McGee *(1983-85; Tri-Capt. '85)*
Anthony Miller *(1986-87)*
Carl Pickens *(1989-91)*
Cory Fleming *(1990-93; Co-Capt. '93)*
Joey Kent *(1993-96)*
Marcus Nash *(1994-97)*
Peerless Price *(1995-98)*

I saw all these cars
with all these orange flags
and I thought Florida was
coming to town.
I'll never make that mistake
again.

Hyatt Regency chef,
New Orleans

Chapter 11

The Fans

The depth of fan loyalty extends far beyond the turnstile count. It displays itself in the throngs that line up two hours before kickoff in all kinds of weather to cheer the team's Walk to the Stadium.

Haywood Harris
Associate A.D. for Media Relations,
University of Tennessee

You were the 12th man on the field. We heard you, and I know Miami heard you.

Chris White
(DB, 1985 Tri-Captain)
to Vol fans welcoming team back home
after 1986 Sugar Bowl upset win

UT has great fans. There are a few obnoxious ones, but by and large they are great fans.

John Tormey
Miami Hurricanes fan,
1986

Tennessee's fans are legendary. Nobody's happier about them being here than the merchants.

Mickey Holmes
Sugar Bowl executive director,
1986

I expect to see the day when Tennessee will send 500 rooters to Nashville to cheer the Volunteers against Vanderbilt, even though their champions have no chance to win.

R.C. "Red" Matthews
UT professor known as the "all-American cheerleader,"
Nov. 13, 1909

The all-important function of college athletics, in these days of strenuous sports, is to instill college spirit into the student body. In many colleges this fails, absolutely. For instance, it is claimed that at Vanderbilt, where the football team is always among the best in the South, the number of students taking interest in the victories of their chosen university is small, comparatively speaking....In the game against Tennessee last Saturday the Gold and Black supporters made almost as much noise as did the few scattered Volunteer rooters. Certainly no more, anyway.

R.C. "Red" Matthews
Nov. 13, 1909

Historic Jackson Square (New Orleans) was the scene and sound of just about any conceivable arrangement and production of "Rocky Top."

John Bibb
sports editor, The Tennessean,
Dec. 31, 1985

I don't try to analyze it. I just make sure that I'm there when the Big Orange plays.

David Keith
actor,
Dec, 28, 1985

I live and die for the Orange. Everybody does.

David Keith

They're not going to beat us because their fans make a lot of noise...

Vinny Testaverde
Miami Hurricanes quarterback,
before being blown out by UT
in the 1986 Sugar Bowl, 35–7

The football season at the University of Tennessee has been about as bad as any in the history of the college, yet this afternoon 500 students are yelling themselves hoarse in the effort to throw the tide of victory to the Volunteers. If this isn't college spirit, then we miss our guess.

> *R.C. "Red" Matthews*
> *Nov. 13, 1909*

It could've been different if we had handled their crowd better. But that's what you have to expect in Knoxville. I learned that a long time ago. When I was in my freshman year as an Alabama player in 1970, we went to Knoxville to play a freshman game. They must've had 35,000 people there for a meaningless game. And they were *loud...*

> *Mike Dubose*
> *Alabama assistant coach,*
> *1984*

We are fortunate in having great fans — students and alumni — who can really get our team ready to play. Our Pride of the Southland Band also is a great contributor to our game efforts.

Bill Battle

There is a happy union of the past, present, and future on autumn Saturdays, when Tennessee fans pour into the huge bowl...some of them literally rising out of the river via the fleet of yachts that dock less than 100 yards from the stadium, many of them shamelessly dressed in the bright golden orange and white that only the football team wore in simpler times.

Ben Byrd

I walked in here and couldn't believe it. It was like we were playing at home. We have such great fans. I swear, I believe if we played in Japan, they'd go over there.

Peerless Price
on seeing the Vol faithful at Vanderbilt Stadium,
Nov. 28, 1998

We've had our fun; now it's time to give our fans a bowl trip they can enjoy.

Tommy Sims
defensive end (1982-85, Tri Capt. '85),
eve of the 1986 Sugar Bowl

They're good, alright.
They even look strong
in the huddle.

Jim Pittman
former Tulane head coach,
on the No. 2-ranked 1967 Vols

Chapter 12

The Teams

The Tennessee squad remains (in Miami) today and tomorrow, breaking training most gentlemanly. They share national honors with TCU and there is glory enough for all. The 1938 Vols will rank as one of the greatest of all Southern teams.

Fred Russell
Nashville Banner,
Jan. 3, 1939,
after Tennessee's 17–0 victory
over Oklahoma in the Orange Bowl

Of the three teams, the 1938 and 1940 were the best, injuries, particularly that of Bad News Cafego, slowing up the 1939 eleven. The 1938 team had great speed and was exceptionally good in its blocking and tackling. Bowden Wyatt, captain and All-America end; Bob Suffridge and Ed Molinski, guards; and Sam Bartholomew, Cafego, Bob Foxx, Babe Wood, and Len Coffman in the backfield were the outstanding players. George Hunter at the other end was also excellent.

Allison Danzig
noted football historian

It's a modern major miracle that we went through the season without having our goal line crossed or a field goal scored.

> *Maj. Robert Neyland*
> *Dec, 9, 1939,*
> *after completion of UT's unbeaten, unscored-upon*
> *1939 regular season — the last college football team*
> *to achieve the feat*

Whether Tennessee is as good as the 1938 Vols is another question. The present Orange machine doesn't pack as much punch. Defensively, the 1939 Vols are as good as last year's team…(but) there is no question that Bowden Wyatt is missed….The main difference between the present Vols and last year is the team play.

> *Raymond Johnson*
> *Nashville Tennessean, Dec. 11, 1939*

I don't believe this 1939 squad ever reached its peak. Not one time has it played the game it was capable of playing. I don't know what it was but we just couldn't get steamed up.

> *Maj. Robert R. Neyland*
> *on his 1939 Vols*

Open the portals of the Rose Bowl, boys, there's a pretty fair country football team heading out that way, the Tennessee Volunteers.

Joe Williams
New York World-Telegram,
1939

For football brains, the squads of the '30s excelled.

Gen. Robert R. Neyland

I honestly think Tennessee would beat any team in the country. That goes for pro teams.

Jock Sutherland
legendary University of Pittsburgh coach (1924-38)

There are several schools in our conference claiming the single wing offense, but there are none who get as much out of it as Tennessee. Frankly, I don't know whether our defensive plans are adequate or not.

Blair Cherry
University of Texas head coach,
before the 15th Cotton Bowl, Jan. 1, 1951.
The Vols won 20–14

This may not be my greatest football team, but it has the greatest courage I've ever seen. We played better football out there today than we know how to play.

> *Gen. Robert R. Neyland*
> *Jan. 1, 1951, after Cotton Bowl triumph over Texas*

We may have "the horse-and-buggy offense," but we've got a dashboard and TV set added.

> *Bowden Wyatt*
> *on his 1956 Vols squad*

While Tennessee teams have been noted for their alertness down through the years, seldom has the university had one that made ball-hawking pay the dividends that this one has. The Vols recovered 21 enemy fumbles during the season and turned 12 of them into touchdowns. They intercepted 16 passes, ran three back for tallies and used seven others to set up scores.

> *Raymond Johnson*
> *on the 1956 Vols*

One thing about the 1967 Vols, they surely weren't lacking in gee-whiz romantics — especially when Richmond Flowers was plucking passes out of the sky.

> *John D. McCallum*

I don't remember a team losing its starting quarterback the fifth game of the season and then going ahead and playing like this (Tennessee) team. On top of that, they don't care who gets the credit. You'd be surprised at what can happen when you think like that.

Frank Broyles
ABC-TV color commentator,
1986 Sugar Bowl pre-game remarks

When we look at the University of Tennessee, we see a team that's playing great football. We see a team that's performing, right now, as well as anybody in the country. We do not see the underdog situation we read about in the papers.

Jimmy Johnson
University of Miami head coach,
1986 Sugar Bowl pre-game remarks

This is probably as fine a football game as I've ever had a team play.

Johnny Majors
after the Vols' 35–7 upset of No. 2-ranked Miami
in the 1986 Sugar Bowl

This is a special team of special men.

Johnny Majors
on his 1985 Vols squad

Destiny, luck, something.

Raynoch Thompson
linebacker,
on the 1998 national champion Vols

Teams have been wearing these orange jerseys with pride for 47 years and trying to accomplish what you accomplished tonight. Remember that. Someday you're going to tell your grandchildren about this.

Phillip Fulmer
to his 1998 Tennessee Vols squad,
after the 23–16 Fiesta Bowl win over Florida State
for the national championship

The one memory I'll never forget —
Waite Field.
It had no sod, but it *did* have a nice
layer of sand and rocky pebbles.

R.T. "Tarzan" Holt
captain, 1923 Vols

Chapter 13

The Fields of Play

Our football field, old Waite Field, was so bad that present-day players would refuse to use it. It was the hardest field one could imagine. Very little, if any, grass would grow on it. Of course what little there was at the beginning of the season was gone before the late games were played. We had to use it for practice and home games. Gravel would wash onto the field from the hillside. I respect and admire those who played under such conditions.

Zora Clevenger

Chilhowee Park & Waite Field

Long before the Orange and White moved onto Shields-Watkins Field (1921), Tennessee football teams, dating as far back as at least 1901, played some of their early games in Chilhowee Park in downtown Knoxville.

After Waite Field, originally a practice field located at 15th and Cumberland, was enlarged, games were played there as well. Before that, around 1906, UT football games were played at Baldwin Park, off Western Ave. in West Knoxville.

When sellout games were played at Waite Field, standing-room-only spectators would watch games from a bank on the east side of the field and from automobiles parked above the field near Ayres Hall.

The north end of Waite Field extended almost to an iron fence that ran along Cumberland Ave. Receivers would understandably shy away from passes thrown into the end-zone vicinity of the fence. At the other end of the field, a part of the south-end end zone was located on a hill, and knowledgeable receivers used the incline to their advantage against unknowing defensive backs. School officials later marked off a curved line in the end zone that made the hill out of bounds to eliminate the offensive advantage.

The grass hadn't come up on the new field yet, and it rained and rained and we were absolutely ankle-deep in mud....I don't know how they expected a man to play on a field that deep in mud. But I'll tell you this: it was like playing on a mattress after playing at old Waite Field with all the rocks and hard places.

Roy "Pap" Striegel
guard (1919-22),
on the new Shields-Watkins Field

Shields-Watkins Field

In 1919, Colonel W.S. Shields, president of the Knoxville City National Bank and a UT trustee, donated $22,453 towards the construction of a new football playing field. The University matched the donation and seven acres were purchased for the project. In return for the generosity extended by Shields and his wife, the former Alice Watkins, UT trustees voted to name the field in their honor.

From the top of the hill where Ayres Hall would later be built, dirt was transported to help fill in a ravine traversing the land tract that had been bought for the playing field. UT Athletic Council chairman and professor of civil engineering Nathan Dougherty, a former Vol standout as a player (1906-09), personally laid out the field himself. Shields would donate another $14,500 for the purchase of additional property. Then a participatory event took place that would be viewed as the rarest of oddities today.

The student body was given a two-day holiday so they could work side-by-side with faculty members, including Dean James Hoskins, who later became UT president, to help level and grade the playing field.

The first sporting event of any kind to take place at Shields-Watkins Field was a baseball game, on March 19, 1921, between Tennessee and Cincinnati. The Vols lost 7–6. That fall, on September 24, the Vols hosted Emory & Henry in the first-ever football game at the facility, a game that Tennessee took 27–0.

I was in awe of it.

Condredge Holloway
on first sight of Neyland Stadium as a UT freshman,
1971

It's not Neyland Stadium.

Johnny Majors
on the Louisiana Superdome

Once they paint that Orange on you, it never washes off.

Harvey Robinson
UT head coach (1953,'54)

Chapter 14

The Orange Crate

Advent of Orange

Up until 1922, Tennessee uniforms featured black jerseys with orange and white bands on the sleeves. It was Vol captain Pap Striegel who, in 1922, suggested to then-head coach M. Beal Banks that a change be made to orange jerseys with white numerals.

However, Bill May, a quarterback on the 1914 SIAA championship team, said he wore an orange jersey for three games, between 1913-15.

Before that Charles Moore, a 150-pound guard on UT's very first official team in 1891, had been credited with selecting the University's orange-and-white color scheme. Moore, it is said, was inspired by the beauty of daisies, which were in prolific number at the time on The Hill.

At any rate, the resultant color change in 1922, first seen in a 50–0 win over Emory & Henry, ushered in what would become one of college football's most distinctive looks in jersey attire.

Some of the All-Time Greats at Linebacker Tech

Mike Lucci *(1960-61; Capt. '61)*
Frank Emanuel *(1963-65)*
Tom Fisher *(1964-65)*
Paul Naumoff *(1964-66; Co-Capt. '66)*
Steve Kiner *(1967-69)*
Jack Reynolds *(1967-69)*
Jackie Walker *(1969-71; Capt. '71)*
Ray Nettles *(1969-71)*
Jamie Rotella *(1970-72; Capt. '72)*
Andy Spiva *(1973-76; Co-Capt. '76)*
Craig Puki *(1975-79; Tri-Capt. '79)*
Dale Jones *(1983-86; Tri-Capt. '86)*
Keith DeLong *(1985-88; Capt. '88)*
Earnest Fields *(1988-91; Co-Capt. '91)*
Darryl Hardy *(1988-91)*
Al Wilson *(1995-1998; Capt. '98)*

Little Dipper Was First Mascot

UT's first mascot was, no, not Smokey, but Little Dipper, an airplane-riding football-cheering canine reared on World War II military missions in the South Pacific.

Little Dipper was the cockpit co-pilot of W.S. "Monk" Fowler, a Vol who won the title "King of the Sub-Killers" while in the Pacific flying Hellcats and other aircraft. The dog was adopted as the official mascot by the Honolulu Navy team with Fowler, later a wingback at UT (1947), at halfback.

Tennessee's better-known mascots — Smokey, a blue-tick coon hound designated as the University's permanent mascot, and the Tennessee Walking Horse — are today's sideline fixtures carrying the Orange and White at UT games. Smokey debuted in 1953; the Walking Horse in 1965.

Single Wing Sayonara

Tennessee's fabled single-wing attack, unrivaled under General Robert Neyland and Bowden Wyatt, was jettisoned by new incoming coach Doug Dickey in 1964. Though the Vols only registered four victories in their initial year with the slot T, Dickey went on to record a glitzy 42–10–3 record the remainder of his six-year tenure in Knoxville.

Suffridge, do your sleeping at the hotel.

Gen. Robert Neyland
after a half-hearted block
thrown by Vols all-time All-America guard Bob Suffridge,
in a pre-1939 Orange Bowl practice

The big boy seems to have a bit of superfluous flesh about his anatomy, but that will not stay after the captain has put him through a few days.

Knoxville Journal
account of overweight UT fullback
Dick "First Down" Dodson
upon reporting to preseason camp in 1925.
The "captain" refers to Coach Neyland's rank
in the military at that time.

Here's wishing you 364 days of success and happiness.

New Year's Day card
sent by the University of Oklahoma football team
to the Tennessee Vols
before the 1939 Orange Bowl game, won by UT 17–0.

I just wish I could wake up two or three hours from now and find out that it was all a bad dream and it's still December 31.

Michael Irvin
University of Miami freshman wide receiver and scorer of
Hurricanes' only TD in 1986 Sugar Bowl loss to Tennessee.

Two-Sport Athletes — A Tennessee Tradition

UT has fashioned its share of remarkable all-around athletes down through the decades. In the late 19th-early 20th century, it was not uncommon for the University's better athletes to compete in a number of sports. But it became more and more of a rarity as skill and proficiency in athletics increased. In addition, sports was becoming "big business." The age of specialization required an athlete to make a choice and play his favorite or best sport. The following are some of the Tennessee athletes who resisted one-sport concentration to excel in two.

Richmond Flowers — All-America in both football and track; missed three world records in track by one-tenth of a second.

Willie Gault — All-America in both football and track; 1980 Olympian in the 400-meter relay.

Anthony Hancock — All-America hurdler.

Mike Miller — All-America sprinter.

Sam Graddy — Olympic and NCAA sprint champion.

Alvin Harper — SEC high jump champion.

Though no official accounts are kept of UT football-baseball athletes, ends **Bert Rechichar** and **Tommy West**, and quarterbacks **Condredge Holloway, Alan Cockrell** and **Todd Helton** all made substantial marks in the diamond dust of Lindsey Nelson Stadium during their careers at Tennessee.

Without rival is four-sport star **Ron Widby** — a football and basketball All-America who also lettered in baseball and golf while a Vol from 1964-66. Widby spent seven years as a punter in the NFL with Dallas and Green Bay.

What I wanted to do was try football (professionally in Canada). If it didn't work out, my plan was to start work immediately on baseball — go to Mexico...South America...wherever I needed to go, and work my way up. Of course, 13 years later, I was still playing football.

— Condredge Holloway
who, as a high school shortstop,
was the No. 1 pick of the Montreal Expos.
Holloway enjoyed a sterling 13-year career
in the Canadian Football League
with the Ottawa Rough Riders (1975-80),
Toronto Argonauts 1981-86),
and the British Columbia Lions (1987),
after his playing days at UT

All those fine ball players...
heck, it'll be hard for me
to make the team
when I get Up There.

Beattie Feathers
reflecting on his 40 years in football
and his old teammates who had passed on

Bibliography
and Index

Bibliography

Anderson, Lars. "High-Voltage Vol." <u>Sports Illustrated Presents</u>. (1/13/99): 41.

Bebb, Russ. <u>The Big Orange</u>. Huntsville, AL: The Strode Publishers, 1973.

Bechtel, Mark. "Scripted to a Tee." <u>Sports Illustrated Presents</u>. (1/13/99): 22, 23, 60, 61, 70.

Bibb, John. <u>The Tennessean</u>. 29 Dec. 1985, 31 Dec. 1985.

Bolton, Clyde. <u>Unforgettable Days in Southern Football</u>. Huntsville, AL: The Strode Publishers, 1974.

Browning, Al. <u>Third Saturday in October</u>. Nashville: Rutledge Hill Press, 1987.

Cawood, Chris. <u>Legacy of the Swamp Rat</u>. Kingston, TN: Magnolia Hill Press, 1994.

Deitsch, Richard. "A Day Like No Other." <u>Sports Illustrated Presents</u>. (1/13/99): 57, 72, 73.

Fields, Bud and Bob Bertucci. <u>A Pictorial History of University of Tennessee Football</u>. West Point, NY: Leisure Press, 1982.

Ford, Bud, ed. <u>1998 University of Tennessee Volunteers Football Guide</u>. Knoxville, TN: Department of Athletics, University of Tennessee, 1998.

Harris, Ed. <u>From T to T at UT</u>. Knoxville, TN: 1963.

Harris, Ed. <u>Golden Memories of Ed Harris: 50 Years in Big Orange Country</u>. Knoxville, TN: 1972.

Johnson, Raymond. <u>The Nashville Tennessean</u>. 11 Dec. 1939, 1 Jan. 1951, 1 Jan. 1957.

Layden, Tim. "At Last: Goodbye, Gators." Sports Illus-
    trated Presents. (1/13/99): 34, 35, 95.

Lucey, Trisha. "Passing Another Test." Sports Illustrated
    Presents. (1/13/99): 42

Maisel, Ivan. "Gotta Start Somewhere." Sports Illus-
    trated Presents. (1/13/99): 28, 79.

McCallum, John D. Southeastern Conference Football.
    New York: Charles Scribner's Sons, 1980.

Mulé, Marty. Sugar Bowl: The First 50 Years. Birming-
    ham, AL: Oxmoor House, Inc., 1983.

Pearlman, Jeff. "General Excellence." Sport Illustrated
    Presents. (1/13/99): 9-10.

Russell, Fred. The Nashville Banner. 3 Jan. 1939, 1 Jan.
    1940, 2 Jan. 1940, 2 Jan. 1968.

Siler, Tom. Thru the Years with the Volunteers. Knox-
    ville, TN: Archer & Smith Printing, Co., 1950.

Siler, Tom. Tennessee's Dazzling Decade, 1960-70.
    Knoxville, TN: Hubert E. Hodge Printing Co., 1970.

Southern Living. "All-South '85". Sept. 1985, pgs. 24s-36s.

Thomsen, Ian. "Saved by a Miracle." Sports Illustrated
    Presents. (1/13/99): 67, 74.

Walters, John. "Tradition, with a Capital 'T'." Sports
    Illustrated Presents. (1/13/99): 46, 47.

Williams, F.M. The Nashville Tennessean. 2 Jan. 1957.

Index

Index

About the Author

Alan Ross is a writer and sports historian living with his wife, Karol, in Monteagle, Tennessee. A graduate of Fordham University, he is a former editor for Professional Team Publications, Athlon Sports Communications, and Walnut Grove Press. His feature articles on sports history have appeared in *The Sporting News*, *Lindy's*, *Athlon Sports*, *Athletic Administration*, *Game Day*, *NFL Insider*, *Arizona Cardinals Media Guide*, *The Coffin Corner*, and *Track Record*. He is also the history columnist for *Titans Exclusive*, the official publication of the NFL's Tennessee Titans.

For information about books from Walnut Grove Press,
call 1-800-256-8584.